Saint Joseph

FIRST
COMMUNION
CATECHISM

Prepared from the Official
Revised Edition of the
Baltimore Catechism

•

CATHOLIC BOOK PUBLISHING CORP.
NEW JERSEY

This Edition is Dedicated to
SAINT JOSEPH
the Foster Father of JESUS
the First Teacher of these truths.

– CONTENTS –

(T-240)

NIHIL OBSTAT: Richard Kugelman, C.P., S.T.L., S.S.L.   *Censor Deputatus*
IMPRIMI POTEST: Gerard Rooney, C.P.   *Provincial*
NIHIL OBSTAT: Eugene F. Richard, M.S.   *Censor Deputatus*
IMPRIMATUR: ✠ Francis Cardinal Spellman   *Archbishop of New York*

© 2012, 1963 by Catholic Book Publishing Corp., NJ — Printed in China — ISBN 978-0-89942-240-4
www.catholicbookpublishing.com   CPSIA   November 2014   10 9 8 7 6 5 4 3 2   L/P

PRAYERS FOR EVERY DAY

In the Name of the Father   and of the Son   and of the Holy   Spirit

The Sign of the Cross

IN THE NAME of the Father,
and of the Son,
and of the Holy Spirit. Amen.

Amen

The Lord's Prayer

OUR FATHER, Who art in heaven,
hallowed be Thy name;
Thy kingdom come,
Thy will be done
on earth as it is in heaven.

Give us this day our daily bread,
and forgive us our trespasses,
as we forgive those who trespass against us;
and lead us not into temptation,
but deliver us from evil. Amen.

The Hail Mary

HAIL, MARY, full of grace!
The Lord is with thee;
blessed art thou among women,
and blessed is the fruit
of thy womb, Jesus.

Holy Mary, Mother of God,
pray for us sinners,
now and at the hour of our death. Amen.

Glory Be to the Father

GLORY BE to the Father,
and to the Son,
and to the Holy Spirit.

As it was in the beginning,
is now, and ever shall be,
world without end. Amen.

Prayer to the Guardian Angel

ANGEL OF GOD,
My Guardian dear,
To whom His love
Entrusts me here,
Ever this day,
Be at my side,
To light and guard,
To rule and guide. Amen.

Morning Offering

O MY GOD, I offer You every thought
and word and act of today.
Please bless me, my God,
and make me good today.

An Act of Faith

O MY GOD, I believe all the truths
which the Holy Catholic Church teaches,
because You have made them known.

An Act of Hope

O MY GOD,
because You are all-powerful,
merciful, and faithful to Your promises,
I hope to be happy with You in heaven.

An Act of Love

O MY GOD,
because You are all-good,
I love You
with my whole heart and soul.

5

GOD MADE ALL THINGS

GOD MADE US

The Purpose of Man's Existence

1. **Who made you?**

   God made me.

God made me out of nothing.
He made me because He loves me.
He gave me to my mother and father.
They take care of me.
They take God's place.
I belong to God because He made me.

2. **Did God make all things?**

   Yes, God made all things.

God made the earth and the sky.
God also made the sun.
God made the moon and the stars.
God made night and day.

God made rain and snow.
God made hills and mountains.
God made oceans and rivers.
God made the trees and flowers.

God made all animals, big and little.
God made the fishes in the water.
God made the birds in the sky.

God made the Angels.
Angels are spirits.
They have no bodies.
They know much more than we do.
They have great power.

The Angel who helps me is my Guardian Angel.
He is with me all the time.
He keeps me from danger.
He helps me to think of God.

God Made Adam and Eve

Adam and Eve were the first man and woman.

God made the sun and moon for them.
God made the trees and flowers for them.
God made the animals for them.
God made the birds and fishes for them.
God made all these things for them to use.
God made the world for all of us.

3. **Why did God make you?**

God made me to show His goodness and to make me happy with Him in heaven.

God Is Good

God made me because He is good.

God is always happy.

God wants everybody to be happy.

God made me to be happy with Him forever.

I cannot be happy without God.

I need God.

Heaven is God's home.

Everybody in heaven is happy.

To be happy forever, we must get to heaven.

Earth is the place where we get ready for heaven.

9

4. **What must you do to be happy with God in heaven?**

To be happy with God in heaven I must know Him, love Him, and serve Him in this world.

First I must KNOW God.
I cannot love God unless I know Him well.
To know God I must study my catechism.
I must think about God every day.
I must pray to God.

Most of all I must LOVE God.
We give gifts to those we love.
I must make my life a gift to God.
I must love God more than I love myself.
I must love God more than I love anybody else.
I must love God above all things.

To show God I love Him I must SERVE Him.
I serve God when I PRAY well.
I try to think of God.

I serve God when I WORK well.
I study hard at school and home.

I serve God when I PLAY well.
I try to be fair and not selfish.

I must not offend God by sin.
I must want to please Him.
It is not always easy to please God.
What pleases Him sometimes does not please us.
I must please God rather than myself.
This shows God I love Him more than myself.

Shall I Be <u>Selfish</u>   **OR**   **Shall I <u>Share</u>**
and PLEASE MYSELF?   **and PLEASE GOD?**

When I am selfish I do not please God.
When I am kind to others I please God.
To be happy I must please God in everything.

CAN YOU ANSWER THESE?

1. Why do you belong to God?
2. Who were the first man and woman?
3. What is God's home called?
4. Why does God want us to come there?
5. What three things must I do to be happy with God?

GOD IS GREAT

God and His Perfections

5. Where is God?

God is everywhere.

God is with us.
God is on earth.
God is in the sky.
God is in all places.
But heaven is God's home.
He also lives in souls that are pleasing to Him.

6. Does God know all things?

Yes, God knows all things.

God knows all things on earth.
God knows all things in heaven.
God knows what happened long ago.
God knows what we are doing now.
God knows what is going to happen.

God knows when we are good.
God knows when we are bad.
God sees all the things we do.

God knows even what we are thinking.
God watches us because He loves us.

He wants to keep us from harm.
He even wants to keep us
   from hurting ourselves.

7. **Can God do all things?**

   Yes, God can do all things.

God can make anything.
God can change anything.
God can change us and make us better,
   if we let Him.

God gives us all the help we need.
God always helps us when we ask Him.
Asking Him to help us is called prayer.

8. **Did God have a beginning?**

   No, God had no beginning. He always was.

The earth had a beginning.
The sun, moon, and stars had a beginning.
The Angels had a beginning.
We had a beginning.

God gave everything a beginning.
Only God had no beginning.
God was never born.

9. Will God always be?

Yes, God will always be.

God can never die.
He will live forever.

1. Where is God's home?

2. What does God know?

3. What can God do?

4. How long will God live?

5. Why does God watch over us?

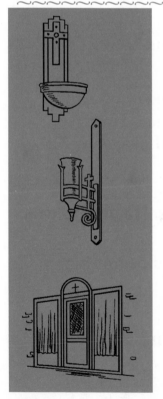

SOME THINGS I SEE IN CHURCH

The **HOLY WATER FONT** is near the door. Holy water is blessed to protect us. I make the Sign of the Cross with it.

The **SANCTUARY LAMP** burns all the time. It burns before Jesus in the Tabernacle. It takes the place of our heart.

The **CONFESSIONAL** is the place where we go to Confession.

THE SON   THE HOLY SPIRIT   THE FATHER

LESSON 3

THE BLESSED TRINITY

The Unity and Trinity of God

10. Is there only one God?

Yes, there is only one God.

There cannot be more than one God.
There never will be more than one God.

11. How many Persons are there in God?

**In God there are three Persons—the
Father, the Son, and the Holy Spirit.**

The Father is God.
The Son is God.
The Holy Spirit is God.
But they are all ONE God.

The Father is the First Person.
The Son is the Second Person.
The Holy Spirit is the Third Person.
There are THREE Persons in ONE God.

15

12. **What do we call the three Persons in one God?**

We call the three Persons in one God the Blessed Trinity.

The Father is God.
The Son is God.
The Holy Spirit is God.
All THREE Persons are ONE God.
We call them the BLESSED TRINITY.

We PICTURE God the Father
   as a kind father.
But He is really a Spirit.
We cannot see a spirit.

SON

FATHER   HOLY SPIRIT

It is easy to PICTURE
   God the Son because He really
   became man.

We PICTURE God the Holy Spirit as a dove.
But He too is really a Spirit.
We also call Him the Holy Ghost.

All three Persons are equal.

13. **How do we know that there are three Persons in one God?**

We know that there are three Persons in one God because we have God's word for it.

The Father sent His Son to us on earth.
The Son told us what the Blessed Trinity is
  like.

The Blessed Trinity is God's family.
But it is a family which is all one God.

In this family all is love.
They never fight.
They always agree.
They are always happy.

Say this prayer often:

O God, make my family holy.

~~~~~~

CAN YOU ANSWER THESE?

1. Is there only one God?
2. How many Persons are there in God?
3. Who are they?
4. Why can't you see God?
5. What do we call all three Persons together?

THE FIRST SINS

Sin: Original Sin

22. What is sin?

Sin is disobedience to God's laws.

God's laws show me the way to heaven.
They are signs that show me the right road.
Sin is saying "No" to God.
It offends God.
Sin shows God I do not love Him very much.

St. Michael Drove the Bad Angels from Heaven

23. Who committed the first sin?

The bad Angels committed the first sin.

All the Angels were made to serve God.
But some loved themselves more than God.
They said, "We will not serve."
They were thrown into hell.
We call them devils.

24. Who committed the first sin on earth?

Our first parents, Adam and Eve, committed the first sin on earth.

God put Adam and Eve in the Garden of Eden.
They were the first people to live on the earth.
God wanted them to be happy.

But He told them not to eat of one tree.

Its fruit would make them die.

The devil spoke to Eve.
He told her the fruit was good.
He told her she would be like God.

Eve Listened to the Devil

Eve did not obey God.
She ate some of the fruit and gave some to Adam.

They loved themselves more than God.

This was the first sin on earth.
They did not believe God.

25. **Is this sin passed on to us from Adam?**

Yes, this sin is passed on to us from Adam.

We are children of Adam and Eve.
They were our first parents.
We are born with this sin on our soul.
We are born without grace in our soul.

26. **What is this sin in us called?**

This sin in us is called original sin.

Original sin means "first" sin.
We are all born with original sin on our souls.
While it is there we cannot love God as He
    loves us.
Baptism washes this sin off our souls.
But original sin leaves our souls weak.
We think more of pleasing ourselves than of
    pleasing God.
We feel like loving ourselves more than God.

Our hearts
turn quickly to
things like:
    Candy
    Toys
    TV
We like them
too much.

Our hearts
turn away from
things like
Obedience
Prayer
Study
But these
please God
more.

**The Effect of Original Sin Is that Our Hearts Are Filled
with Love for Ourselves.**

27. Was anyone ever free from original sin?

The Blessed Virgin Mary was free from original sin.

God wanted to free everybody from sin.
To do this, He planned to send His Son to earth.
He wanted His Son to have a good mother.
So He made the best mother He could.

God made Mary.
He kept her free from
  original sin.
She came into the world
  without it.
She never had sin.

Mary's soul was always
  turned to God.
Her heart was always
  full of love for God.
She was full of grace.

**The Blessed Virgin Mary
with Her Mother, Saint Anne**

We call this Mary's IMMACULATE CONCEPTION.

Even as a baby, Mary's heart loved God.
She grew up loving God.
She did not love herself more than God.
She wanted only to please God.
She always did what God wanted.

An Angel Gave Mary God's Message

God sent an Angel to see Mary.
He asked her to be the Mother of Jesus.

Mary said "Yes" to the Angel.

God sent His Son to her.
God made her the Mother of Jesus.
He did this by the power of the Holy Spirit.
Mary prepared Jesus to die on the Cross for us.

CAN YOU ANSWER THESE?

1. What does a sinner say to God?
2. What did Adam and Eve say to God?
3. What did Mary say to God?

22

OUR OWN SINS

Actual Sin

28. Is original sin the only kind of sin?

No, there is another kind of sin, called actual sin.

Adam and Eve committed **ORIGINAL** sin.
We did not commit it, but are born with it.
The sin <u>we</u> commit is **ACTUAL** sin.

29. What is actual sin?

Actual sin is any sin which we ourselves commit.

Actual Sin Is Doing Wrong

We are not born with actual sin.
We commit it **ourselves.**

30. How many kinds of actual sin are there?

There are two kinds of actual sin: mortal sin and venial sin.

23

31. What is mortal sin?

Mortal sin is a deadly sin.

It is a big sin committed on purpose.
The word **deadly** means that it kills our soul.

Children do not often commit mortal sin.
God protects them in a special way.
But big people sometimes commit mortal sin.
Even big boys and girls do sometimes.
We must hate mortal sin.

32. What does mortal sin do to us?

Mortal sin makes us enemies of God and robs our souls of His grace.

Anyone who commits mortal sin loves himself
   more than God.
He offends God very much.
One whose soul is dead in sin has no power to
   love God.
He cannot please God.

GRACE is the life
   of Christ in us.

Mortal sin kills
   this life.

It CRUCIFIES
   CHRIST in us.

Grace in the Soul
Christ lives in us.

Mortal Sin in the Soul
Christ is crucified in us.

33. **What happens to those who die in mortal sin?**

Those who die in mortal sin are punished forever in the fire of hell.

Hell is a terrible place.

Those who are there suffer great pain.

They are slaves of the devil.

They hate God and everyone else.

They love only themselves.

They can never be happy.

34. **What is venial sin?**

Venial sin is a lesser sin.

Mortal sin is doing something big that God does not like.

Venial sin is doing something not so big that God does not like.

Sometimes we commit venial sin on purpose.

Sometimes we commit it without thinking.

If we do it on purpose, it offends God.

If we do it without thinking, it does not offend God.

But we must be sorry afterward and try to find out why we committed the sin.

35. **Does venial sin make us enemies of God or rob our souls of His grace?**

No, venial sin does not make us enemies of God or rob our souls of His grace.

Venial sin does not kill God's life in our souls.
But it makes our souls sick.
Our soul is more important
    than our body.
It is worse to have a sick soul
    than a sick body.

Our Blessed Lord loves us.
Venial sin makes Him SAD,
    if we do it on **purpose**,
    or do not try to do **better**.

Venial Sin in the Soul
Christ is sad in us.

36. **Does venial sin displease God?**

Yes, venial sin does displease God.

God loves you.
Venial sin hurts your own soul.
It displeases God to see you hurt yourself.
Does your mother like to see you hurt yourself?

CAN YOU ANSWER THESE?
1. What sin do we commit ourselves?
2. What does mortal sin do to the life of Christ in us?
3. What sin makes our soul sick?
4. Why should we hate sin?

THE SON OF GOD BECOMES MAN

The Incarnation

14. **Did one of the Persons of the Blessed Trinity become man?**
Yes, the Second Person, the Son of God, became man.

15. **What is the name of the Son of God made man?**
The name of the Son of God made man is Jesus Christ.

His name is holy.

We bow our heads when we say or hear His name.

Jesus, I love You.

27

16. **When was Jesus born?**

Jesus was born on the first Christmas Day, more than two thousand years ago.

Christmas is the birthday of Jesus Christ.
He was born in a stable in Bethlehem.
On Christmas we are happy, because it is the
    birthday of Jesus.
He became a baby for us.
He likes to be with us.

Jesus Was Born in a Stable

17. Who is the Mother of Jesus?

The Mother of Jesus is the Blessed Virgin Mary.

Mary was His Mother on earth.
Jesus had no father on earth.
He had a Father in heaven.
But Saint Joseph took the place of the Father in heaven.
We call Saint Joseph the foster father of Jesus.

18. Is Jesus Christ both God and man?

Yes, Jesus Christ is both God and man.

Jesus Christ is God.
Jesus Christ is man.
Jesus Christ is God and man.

Jesus Christ is the Son of God.
Jesus Christ is the Son of Mary.
Jesus Christ is like His heavenly Father.
Jesus Christ is like us as man.

~~~~~~

CAN YOU ANSWER THESE?

1. Who is Jesus Christ?
2. Where was He born?
3. What do we call His birthday?
4. Who is His Mother?
5. Who is Saint Joseph?

JESUS OPENS HEAVEN FOR US

The Redemption — The Church

19. Why did God the Son become man?

God the Son became man to satisfy for the sins of all men and to help everybody to gain heaven.

God loves all men.
God wanted all men in heaven.
God sent His Son to show men the way.
God sent His Son to open the gates of heaven.

Jesus said: "I am the WAY, and the TRUTH, and the LIFE. No one comes to the FATHER but through ME." (John 14:6)

20. How did Jesus satisfy for the sins of all men?

Jesus satisfied for the sins of all men by His sufferings and death on the Cross.

The Gates of Heaven Had Been Closed by Sin

The sin of Adam and Eve had closed them.
God sent His Son Jesus to make up for sin.
God sent His Son because He loves us.

Jesus died on the Cross for us.
He died because He loved His Father.
He died because He loved us.

Love pleases God.   Sin displeases God.

The love of Jesus pleased the Father **more** than sin displeased Him.

31

THE LOVE OF JESUS . . . DESTROYED THE POWER OF SIN

The LOVE of Jesus was like a fire in His Heart.
Jesus lit this fire in Mary's heart too.
This love made Jesus die on the Cross for us.
This love pleased the Father more than sin displeased Him.
Sin lost its power to keep us out of heaven.

32

THE LOVE OF JESUS . . . OPENED THE GATES OF HEAVEN

The Father in heaven was PLEASED with this love.
So He raised the body of His Son from the dead.
He opened the gates of heaven to welcome His Son.
Mary gave Jesus to the Father for us.
Jesus went home to heaven to prepare a place for us.

The Church Is Our Ladder to Heaven

21. How does Jesus help all men to gain heaven?

Jesus helps all men to gain heaven through the Catholic Church.

The Church is like a ladder to heaven.

Jesus gave us only ONE ladder.

The Church is our only way to heaven.

~~~~~~~~~~~~~~~~~~~~~~~~~~~~~~~~~~~~~~

CAN YOU ANSWER THESE?

1. What kept the gates of heaven closed?
2. Who died to pay for our sins?
3. What pleased the Father more than sin displeased Him?
4. Where did Jesus go after He rose from the dead?

34

THE SACRAMENTS OF BAPTISM AND CONFIRMATION

1. BAPTISM

37. How does the Catholic Church help us to gain heaven?

The Catholic Church helps us to gain heaven especially through the Sacraments.

The Sacraments Are Steps to Heaven

The Church is our ladder to heaven.
The Sacraments are the seven steps of the ladder.
God lets the ladder down.
Our Lady helps us up the ladder.

35

38. What is a Sacrament?

A Sacrament is an outward sign, instituted by Christ to give grace.

A SACRAMENT is a SIGN of Christ.

It is Christ working in our soul.
It is Christ helping our soul.
Christ is hidden in every Sacrament.

39. What does grace do to the soul?

Grace makes the soul holy and pleasing to God.

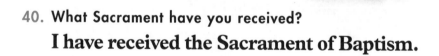

Grace is life.
It is God's life.
It is Christ in us.
It makes our souls
   look like Christ.
It gives us power to please God.

40. What Sacrament have you received?

I have received the Sacrament of Baptism.

41. What did Baptism do for you?

Baptism washed away original sin from my soul and made it rich in the grace of God.

Baptism Is a Second Birth

Baptism is birth.
By it we are born of God.
He sends His Son into our soul.

God becomes our Father too.
Mary becomes our Mother.
The Holy Spirit pours grace into us.

Baptism washes us from original sin.
It drives away the devil.
He can no longer hurt us unless we let him.

42. Are you preparing to receive other Sacraments?

I am preparing to receive the Sacraments of Penance, Holy Eucharist, and Confirmation.

2. CONFIRMATION

43. What will Confirmation do for you?

Confirmation, through the coming of the Holy Spirit, will make me a soldier of Jesus Christ.

Every Sacrament gives us the Holy Spirit.
It gives us more of His power.

Confirmation gives us power to help others to
 know about Jesus.
It gives us **strength** to suffer for Jesus.
It helps us to die for our faith if we have to.
We must be willing to die for Jesus.
Jesus died for us.

Confirmation Gives Power to Spread the Faith

CAN YOU ANSWER THESE?

1. Who is hidden in every Sacrament?
2. What does He do there?
3. What is grace?
4. When does God become our Father?
5. What does Confirmation help us to do?

~~~~~~

SOME THINGS TO HELP ME PRAY

The **ROSARY** is like a crown of roses.
On each big bead we say an "Our Father."
On each little bead we say a "Hail Mary."
We give them all to Our Lady.
She is pleased with them.

A **PRAYER BOOK** helps me pray.
It tells me what to say to God.
God likes me to talk to Him.
I do not always need a book to pray.

HOLY PICTURES remind me of God and the Saints.
I must not play with them.
I must take care of them.

39

THE SACRAMENT OF PENANCE

44. What is the Sacrament of Penance?

Penance is the Sacrament by which sins committed after Baptism are forgiven.

Mortal sin kills the life of Christ in our soul.
Venial sin makes our soul sick.
The Sacrament of Penance is like medicine.
It is the medicine of Christ's Precious Blood.
It cures sick souls.
It is much stronger than medicine for the body.
It even raises dead souls to life.

Jesus said to the man who could not walk, "Your sins are forgiven. Arise and go to your house." And the man got up and walked. (See Luke 5:20-24.)

This Sacrament heals the wounds of all our sins.
It helps us to be good afterward.
It helps us to keep out of sin.

Our sins may be big.
Our sins may be many.
But Our Lord always forgives us if we are sorry.
He is never angry with us.
He loves to have us come to Confession.

45. **What must you do to receive the Sacrament of Penance worthily?**

   To receive the Sacrament of Penance worthily I must:

   1. Find out my sins.

   2. Be sorry for my sins.

   3. Make up my mind not to sin again.

   4. Tell my sins to the priest.

   5. Do the penance the priest gives me.

The best way to do this is:

   Pray to the Holy Spirit.
   Then think about Our Lord's sufferings.

We call these sufferings His Passion.

**BEFORE CONFESSION
THINK ABOUT THE PASSION**

Our sins made Jesus suffer.
He suffered in our place.
We should have been on the Cross.
He did not commit the sins; we did.
But He loves us.
He wanted to suffer for our sins.

When we see His hands and feet nailed,
   we will be sorry we did that to Him.
When we see His bleeding Body,
   we will make up our mind not to sin again.
When we see His face,
   we will want to tell our sins to the priest.
When we see His eyes,
   we will want to say our penance.

DID I COMMIT ANY OF THESE SINS?

Did I miss Mass on purpose on a Sunday or Holy Day? (*Number of times*)

Was I late for Mass on Sunday through my own fault? (. . . . *times*)

Did I laugh or talk in church? (. . . . *times*)

Was I disobedient to others? (. . . . *times*)

Did I talk back to them? (. . . . *times*)

Did I fight with someone? (. . . . *times*)

Did I use angry words? (. . . . *times*)

Did I try to get even with someone? (. . . . *times*)

Did I use bad words? (. . . . *times*)

Did I steal something? (. . . . *times*)

Did I tell any lies? (. . . . *times*)

Was I unkind to others? (. . . . *times*)

Did I call anyone bad names? (. . . . *times*)

Was I mean to others? (. . . . *times*)

Did I tease someone unkindly? (. . . . *times*)

~~~~~~

CAN YOU ANSWER THESE?

1. What Sacrament heals our sick souls?
2. What medicine does it use?
3. If we ever have big sins, will Our Lord forgive us?
4. Is He angry with us?
5. What is the best way to get ready for Confession?

LESSON 10

HOW TO MAKE A GOOD CONFESSION

46. How do you make your Confession?

I make my Confession in this way:

1. I go into the confessional and kneel.

2. I make the Sign of the Cross and say: "Bless me, Father, for I have sinned."

3. I say: "This is my first Confession"* (or, "It has been one week, or one month, since my last Confession").

4. I confess my sins.

5. I listen to what the priest tells me.

6. I say the Act of Contrition loud enough for the priest to hear me.

"This is my first Confession" need not be taught if there is danger that the children will continue to repeat it in subsequent Confessions.

The Priest Takes Christ's Place

Remember you are talking to Our Lord.
Do not be afraid. Tell the truth.
Tell all the sins you can remember.
Do not leave out any sin on purpose.
If you forget to tell a sin, God forgives you.
Listen carefully to the priest.
Say your Act of Contrition from your heart.

47. **What do you do after leaving the confessional?**

After leaving the confessional, I say the penance the priest has given me and thank God for forgiving my sins.

Thanksgiving after Confession

Look at the crucifix again.
Thank Our Lord for His sufferings.
Thank Him for curing your sins.
Say your penance from your heart.
Ask Jesus to help you to be better.

CAN YOU ANSWER THESE?

1. What is the first thing you say in Confession?

2. What do you say about your last Confession?

3. What do you do next?

4. What do you do after the priest gives you your penance?

PRAYER BEFORE CONFESSION	PRAYER AFTER CONFESSION
COME, HOLY SPIRIT, give me Your light to see my sins, and give me Your help to be sorry for them. Show me why I sinned. Help me never again to sin on purpose.	MY JESUS, I thank You for washing away my sins in Your Precious Blood. Help me to accept my cross each day and not to hurt You. I love You with my whole heart and soul.

SIGNS OR SYMBOLS OF CHRIST I SEE IN CHURCH

A cross should remind me that Our Lord died on the Cross for me.

The letters "I H S" mean JESUS in Greek. This was a language used when Jesus was on earth.

The letters "P" and "X", placed one over the other, mean CHRIST in Greek.

Next time you are in church, see how many of these symbols you can find.

46

THE HOLY EUCHARIST

The Last Supper Was the First Mass

48. What is the Sacrament of the Holy Eucharist?

The Holy Eucharist is the Sacrament of the Body and Blood of Our Lord Jesus Christ.

The Holy Eucharist is Our Lord Himself.
He comes to us in Person.
He comes to be Food for our soul.
He comes to live in us.
He comes to stay with us.
He comes to help us always.

49. When does Jesus Christ become present in the Holy Eucharist?

Jesus Christ becomes present in the Holy Eucharist during the Sacrifice of the Mass.

THE MASS IS OUR GIFT TO GOD

We offer bread and wine.
The priest does it for us.
We give our hearts to God.

Then the priest changes
the bread and wine.
They become the Body
and Blood of Jesus.

The priest offers
them to God.

This tells **God**
we love Him.

Jesus offers Himself as He did on the Cross.
We also offer ourselves with Jesus.
We are willing to suffer with Him.

The Gift of Jesus on the Cross pleased the
  Father,
    so the Father raised Jesus from the dead.

Our Gift at Mass pleases the Father too,
    so the Father will raise us with Jesus.
Some day we will all be together in heaven.

50. **Do you receive Jesus Christ in the Sacrament of the Holy Eucharist?**

I do receive Jesus Christ in the Sacrament of the Holy Eucharist when I receive Holy Communion.

To show He is pleased, the Father invites us to
  His table.

He gives us something to eat.

He gives us what we have given Him.

He gives us the Flesh and Blood of His Son.

He gives us the Host which looks like bread,
  but which is JESUS CHRIST.

Jesus Christ is the Food and Drink of our soul.

It makes our souls **strong**.

51. Do you see Jesus Christ in the Holy Eucharist?

No, I do not see Jesus Christ in the Holy Eucharist because He is hidden under the appearances of bread and wine.

The **Eucharist** is **Christ.**
He is really there.
We cannot see Him.
We cannot hear Him.
But He is there.

The HOST looks like bread.
But it **is really** the **Body of Jesus**.
The big Host is for the priest.
The small Hosts are for the people.

Each Host is **Jesus.**

The CHALICE contains the **Blood.**
It looks and tastes like wine.
But it **is really** the **Blood of Jesus.**

The Mass is an act of love.
Our Lord says to His Father, "I love You."
He tells this to the Father for us.
He wants us to say it with Him.

52. What must you do to receive Holy Communion?

To receive Holy Communion I must:

1. Have my soul free from mortal sin.

2. Not eat or drink anything for one hour before Holy Communion. But water may be taken at any time before Holy Communion.

People in mortal sin may not go to Communion.
It is a big sin if they go.
The life of Christ in their souls is **dead.**
Dead people cannot eat.

But sick people need to eat.
Venial sin makes the soul **sick.**
We can receive Communion with venial sins.
But first we should be sorry for our sins.

I must not eat for **one** hour before
   Communion.
I must not drink anything for one hour.
I may take water or medicine any time.
All this is to show respect for Our Lord.

53. What should you do before Holy Communion?

Before Holy Communion I should:

1. Think of Jesus.

2. Say the prayers I have learned.

3. Ask Jesus to come to me.

54. What should you do after Holy Communion?

After Holy Communion I should:

1. Thank Jesus for coming to me.

2. Tell Him how much I love Him.

3. Ask Him to help me.

4. Pray for others.

Then thank Him, talk to Him, ask His help.

CAN YOU ANSWER THESE?

1. Who comes to live in us at Communion time?

2. Why does He come to us?

3. Who offers the Mass for us?

4. What do the bread and wine at Mass become?

5. What does Jesus say to His Father at Mass?

PRAYER BEFORE COMMUNION	PRAYER AFTER COMMUNION
MY JESUS, I need You. It is hard for me to be good.	MY JESUS, I love You. Stay with me always.
Come to make my soul strong.	I need Your help to be good.
Give my soul its Food and Drink.	Change what is bad in me.
Let me grow in Love for You.	Make me just like You.

THE HOLY MASS

THE MASS IS CHRIST'S ACT OF LOVE

Our Lord faces <u>two</u> ways at Mass.

1. He looks up to heaven.

   He gives Himself to the Father in love.

   And we give ourselves with Him.

2. He looks at us.

   He gives us His own Body and Blood.

   They are Food and Drink for our souls.

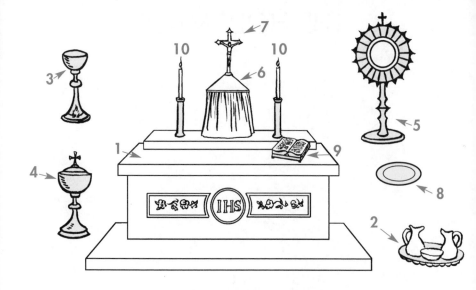

THINGS I SEE AT THE ALTAR

1. The **ALTAR** is a table. Mass is said on it. It is very holy.

2. The **CRUETS** contain the wine and water to be used at the Preparation of the Gifts.

3. The **CHALICE** is a cup which holds Our Lord's Precious Blood at Mass.

4. The **CIBORIUM** is a cup which holds the Hosts the people receive at Communion.

5. The **MONSTRANCE** is a shrine where Our Lord's Body is placed so people can see and adore Him.

6. The **TABERNACLE** is like a tent. Our Lord lives in it.

7. The **CRUCIFIX** is a cross with Our Lord on it. It reminds us He died for us. He loved us so much to do this.

8. The **PATEN** or plate holds the bread to be consecrated by the priest.

9. The **MISSAL** is a big prayer book, with prayers of the Mass. It rests on a stand on the altar.

10. The **CANDLES** remind us of Our Lord. They are made of pure wax. They burn like His Sacred Heart.

54

THE BEGINNING OF MASS

THE PRIEST AT THE FOOT OF THE ALTAR

The priest begins the Mass.
He tells God he is sorry for his sins.
We tell God we are sorry for our sins too.

O God, I am sorry for my sins.
Help me to do better.
Help me to pay attention to the
Mass.

THE PRIEST AT THE MISSAL
AND AT THE LITURGY OF THE WORD

He praises God.
He prays for our needs.
He reads God's words to us.
On Sundays he preaches a sermon.

O my God, we adore You.
Thank You for Your love.
Help us to be good.
Teach us what we should know.

THE PRIEST OFFERS BREAD AND WINE

He offers the bread to God.
He puts wine in the chalice.
He offers that to God.

O God, we offer ourselves to You.
We put our hearts in the chalice.
We want to please You always.

CONSECRATION OF THE HOST

This is the most important part of
the Mass.
The priest bends low over the bread.
The people kneel in silence.
The priest says the words of Christ,

THIS IS MY BODY.

The bread is changed into Christ's
Body.

O God, we love You.

We offer You our gift of
bread.

Our hearts are in it.

Change the bread into the
Body of Your Son.

Change our hearts too.

Fill them with love for You.

ELEVATION OF THE HOST

The priest genuflects.
He raises the Host for all to see.
The people look up and adore Jesus.
Say:

MY LORD AND MY GOD!

CONSECRATION OF THE CHALICE

Now the priest bends over the chalice.

He says the words of Christ,

THIS IS THE CHALICE OF MY BLOOD.

The wine is changed into Christ's Blood.

It reminds us of His death on the Cross.

It is really the same Act of Love.

O God, we love You.

We offer You the Blood of Your Son.

He shed it for us.

Please accept our gift.

ELEVATION OF THE CHALICE

The priest genuflects.

He raises the chalice for all to see.

The people look up and adore the Precious Blood.

Say:

MY JESUS, MERCY!

THE OUR FATHER

The priest is getting ready for Communion.
He says the "Our Father."
He asks the Father for the daily Bread of
the Eucharist.

OUR Father,
who art in heaven,
hallowed be Thy name;
Thy kingdom come,
Thy will be done
on earth as it is in heaven.
Give us this day our daily bread,
and forgive us our trespasses,
As we forgive those
who trespass against us;
And lead us not into temptation,
but deliver us from evil. Amen.

THE COMMUNION

The priest receives the Host.
He drinks the Precious Blood.
The people eat the Bread of Life.

Dear Lord, make us worthy
to receive You.
Take away our power to sin.
Give our souls their Food and
Drink.
Make us strong in love for
You.
Lead us to life everlasting.

LIVING THE MASS

We must LIVE our Mass each day.

To live the Mass we must love and suffer as Jesus did.

TO LOVE

Jesus loved everybody.

We must love everybody.

We must be kind to all.

The Mass helps us to love the way Jesus did.

TO SUFFER

Jesus suffered for us.

We must suffer for and with Him.

To suffer means to do what we don't like to do when God wants it.

The Mass helps us to suffer with Jesus.

THE TWO BIGGEST FEASTS OF THE YEAR

EASTER SUNDAY
The day Our Lord rose from the dead.

PENTECOST SUNDAY
The day the Holy Spirit descended on the Apostles.

HOLY DAYS OF OBLIGATION

THE IMMACULATE
CONCEPTION–December 8

This Feast reminds us how holy Mary's body and soul were made by God.

THE ASCENSION
(40 days after Easter)

The day Our Lord went up to heaven.

CHRISTMAS–December 25

This is Our Lord's birthday.

ASSUMPTION–August 15

The day Our Lady was taken up to heaven.

MARY, THE HOLY MOTHER
OF GOD–January 1

The day when Our Lord received His name Jesus.

ALL SAINTS–November 1

The day we think of all the Saints in heaven.

VARIOUS PRAYERS

The Blessing before Meals

BLESS US, O Lord, and these Thy gifts which we are about to receive from Thy bounty, through Christ Our Lord. Amen.

Grace after Meals

WE GIVE THEE THANKS for all Thy benefits, O Almighty God, who lives and reigns forever. Amen. May the souls of the faithful departed, through the mercy of God, rest in peace. Amen.

Ejaculations

MY Jesus, mercy.
Most Sacred Heart of Jesus, have mercy on us.

Mother of mercy, pray for us.

Jesus, Mary, and Joseph,
bless us now and at the hour of our death.

NIGHT AND OTHER PRAYERS

MY GOD and Father,
I thank You for all the blessings
You have given me today.
I am sorry for all my sins,
because they have hurt You,
my dearest Father.

An Act of Contrition

O MY GOD, I am sorry for all my sins,
because of Thy just punishments,
and because they displease Thee,
Who art all-good and deserving of all my love.
With Thy help, I will sin no more.

62

Another Act of Contrition (Longer Form)

O MY God, I am heartily sorry
    for having offended Thee,
  and I detest all my sins,
  because of Thy just punishments,
  but most of all,
  because they offend Thee, my God,
  Who art all good and deserving of all my love.
I firmly resolve,
    with the help of Thy grace,
    to sin no more
    and to avoid the near occasions of sin. Amen.

The Confiteor

I CONFESS to Almighty God,
  to blessed Mary ever Virgin,
  to blessed Michael the Archangel,
  to blessed John the Baptist,
  to the holy Apostles Peter and Paul,
  and to all the saints,
  that I have sinned exceedingly
  in thought, word, and deed,
  through my fault, through my fault,
  through my most grievous fault.
Therefore,
  I beseech blessed Mary ever-Virgin,
  blessed Michael the Archangel,
  blessed John the Baptist, the holy Apostles
  Peter and Paul, and all the Saints,
  to pray to the Lord our God for me.
May the Almighty God have mercy on me,
  and forgive me my sins,
  and bring me to everlasting life. Amen.
May the Almighty and merciful Lord
  grant me pardon, absolution,
  and remission of all my sins. Amen.

The
Apostles'
Creed

I BELIEVE in God,
the Father almighty,
Creator of heaven and earth,
and in Jesus Christ, His only Son,
  Our Lord,
Who was conceived by the
  Holy Spirit,
born of the Virgin Mary,
suffered under Pontius Pilate,
was crucified, died, and was buried;
He descended into hell;
on the third day He rose again from
  the dead;
He ascended into heaven,
and is seated at the right hand of God
  the Father almighty;
from there He will come to judge
  the living and the dead.

I believe in the Holy Spirit,
the holy catholic Church,
the communion of saints,
the forgiveness of sins,
the resurrection of the body,
and life everlasting. Amen.